This book belongs to

 ·

Our New Baby

MEMORY BOOK

Illustrated by Antonia Woodward

Waiting...

Before you were born, we waited for you.
You grew, wriggled, and hiccupped night and day
and we wondered who you would be.

ultrasound scan picture

You were....... weeks in this picture.

All about you

You've arrived! Welcome to God's wonderful world, brand new person.

We named you
. . . .

You were born at
. . . .

(time)
. . . .

(date)
. . . .

(home/name of hospital)
. . . .

(place)
. . . .

This is the story of YOU!

first photo/day of birth photo

Your first photo.

baby's hospital name band

Your hospital name band.

When you were born

You weighed

. . . .

Your length was

. . . .

Your eyes were

. . . .

Your hair was

. . . .

You looked like

. . . .

We thank God for your safe journey into the world, little one.

Dear God, you know all about me,
You created me inside and out,
I am beautifully and wonderfully made,
You know all my days ahead and
you will keep me safe.

Psalm 139, the Bible

photo of you

Our family

This is your family tree

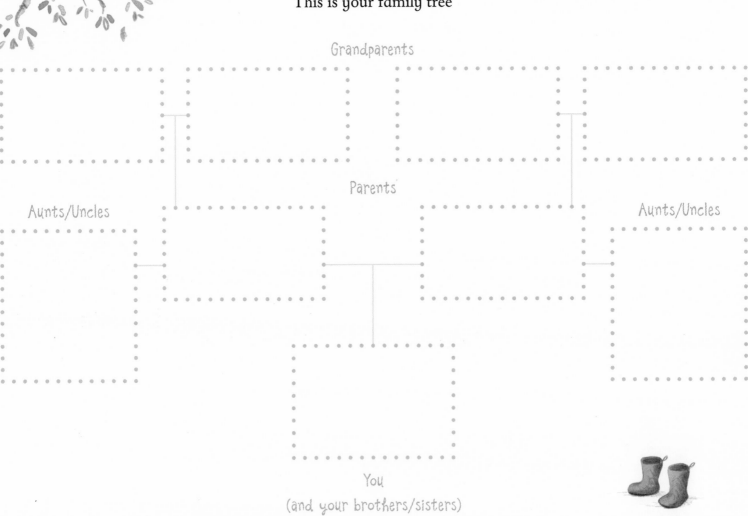

Grandparents

Parents

Aunts/Uncles

Aunts/Uncles

You
(and your brothers/sisters)

The people in your family are:

· ·

· ·

· ·

· ·

· ·

· ·

photo of family members

photo of family friends

Family and friends are the home we grow up in.

photo of you and your family

Your family has changed now that you are here. We are different because of you.
There is no one in the whole world as wonderful as you. You are special.
We will surround you with tenderness and love every day.

Your first home

When you were a baby we lived at

· ·

· ·

You slept in   (basket/cot)
· ·

and you lay   (baby's sleeping position)
· ·

You had your first bath on
· ·

You   (baby's reaction)
· ·
during your bath.

Our special place to sit and hold you was
· ·

This home is our rest and refuge, a safe shelter for honest tears and joyful laughter.

photo of your home

Like a bird, God will cover you with his feathers. Under his wings you will be safe.

Psalm 91, the Bible

photo of you playing

You liked to

....

You played with

....

You listened to

....

You liked the smell of

....

You liked the sound of

....

You slept .... (times of day)

....

You liked the touch of

....

You had your first injections on

....

Your first day trip was

. . . .

and we saw

. . . .

You cried a lot when

. . . .

You first smiled at

. . . .

photo of you on your first day trip out

photo of you smiling

Your first achievements

You grew and changed, learning to do new things each day.

This month you

· ·

· ·

You first rolled over in   (month)
· ·

You reached out for a toy in   (month)
· ·

You first held your bottle in   (month)
· ·

photo of you playing with your toys

Your first achievements

This month...

You babbled and said
. . . .

You sat up on your own   (where and when)
. . . .

You began to crawl for the first time on
. . . .

You took your very first steps on
. . . .

with   (who)
. . . .

photo of you walking

Your first achievements

photo of you swimming

God says 'Do not be afraid, I am with you. I will make you strong and help you.'

Isaiah, the Bible.

Your first solid food was

....

on

....

Your first time to be unwell was

....

Your first tiny tooth popped through

....

Your first drink from a cup was

....

You slept through the whole night on

....

You had your first swim on

....

Special days

Your family and friends gathered together for a very important day on

. . . .

. . . .

We welcomed you into our church family at

. . . .

and celebrated God's amazing gift to us, you!

We asked God to bless your life, for now and always.

photo or stick in the invitation to Baptism/Christening/Naming day

photos from your Baptism/Christening/Naming day

God's Word is a lamp to light up the way for my life.

Psalm 119, the Bible

The people who came to your special day were

....

....

....

....

....

Your Godparents are

....

....

Dear God,

Thank you for putting wise grown-ups
and children in my life. Please keep them
safe and bless them.

Prayers, promises, and blessings from all those who love you, little one.

Your First birthday

On .... (date)

you turned 1. You've grown up so much. We celebrated your birthday by

....

....

....

....

Your handprint

Your favourite things

Toy
....

Book
....

Word/Sound
....

Friend
....

Place
....

Blanket
....

photo of you with your favourite things

photo of you

Baby

....

(name)

You are a treasure to us, little one. We love you when you are grumpy or upset, we love you when you
are bouncy and joyful, noisy or gentle. No matter what or where or when, we will always love you.

. . . .

. . . .